Assess Your Own Teaching Quality

Teaching and Learning in Higher Education Series
Series Editor: John Stephenson

Assess Your Own Teaching Quality

Sally Brown and Phil Race

KOGAN PAGE

London • Philadelphia

To our respective (but not respectful) sons, Matt, Pete and Angus

First published in 1995
Reprinted 1996, 1997

Kogan Page Limited
120 Pentonville Road
London N1 9JN

British Library Cataloguing in Publication Data

A CIP record for this book is available from the British Library.

ISBN 0 7494 1370 0

Typeset by Saxon Graphics Ltd, Derby
Printed and bound in Great Britain by Biddles Ltd, Guildford and King's Lynn

Contents

Preface and Acknowledgements

'First, know thyself'

We have written this book as much as a self-appraisal device to use in our own teaching as for colleagues to use in theirs. Our book is meant to be a friend, not an enemy. We should say here that we don't imagine for a moment that we manage to live up to all the checklist criteria contained in this book. All we claim is to have identified some criteria which we would like to move closer to in our work; we know that we could never fulfil all of them.

We are on the side of the appraisee. Equally, we are on the side of the learner, and on the side of the learner that is inside all good teachers. We are committed to a continuous cycle of self-evaluation in our professional lives to ensure that we continue to learn and develop.

This book is a creative response to some of the pressures that both ourselves and our colleagues are experiencing as teaching quality assessments are conducted at our institutions, and as appraisal systems are implemented in our profession. The pressures on us all are increased by the fact that in many of our courses we are having to accommodate greater numbers of students, often with the same resources and staff.

We recognize in this book that 'teaching quality' is a term which should embrace a wide range of the professional activities that lecturers engage in in their everyday work, not just the recognized tasks of lecturing and tutoring. We have tried to include a wide range of activities in our checklists, but we cannot claim to have covered everything! There are many more dimensions to good teaching than we have addressed here, and some dimensions which we have addressed will repay further attention to that we have been able to give them.

We do not regard our work as finished; new checklist criteria, new issues, better criteria will continue to emerge. We invite you to let us know how we can make this book more useful.

Acknowledgements

We thank numerous colleagues and workshop participants at many locations in the United Kingdom and Germany who have given us feedback on components of this book during the time we were developing and trialling them. We would particularly like to thank a number of colleagues who have helped us enormously by providing feedback on the pilot edition of our book: Brenda Smith, Teaching Quality Manager, Nottingham Trent University; Peter Dove and Liz McDowell, Educational Development Advisors, University of Northumbria at Newcastle; and Gus Pennington, Head of the Educational Development Service, University of Teesside.

Introduction

How *not* to use this book!

Please don't try to read this book from cover to cover and give yourself a mark out of 500! This book lists more than 500 'affirmations of quality of teaching', but don't expect to check off all of these, however experienced you are – no one is that good! All of the statements in the checklists may represent desirable practice, but in our professional practice all any of us can hope for is to achieve a significant number of them (and to be aware of some of those we don't achieve). So please don't look at this book as a list of all the things you should be achieving *now* in your work. It is our intention that you should use it as a means to reflect on the areas of your work where you are already successful, and to work out your own agenda for those parts of your work where you wish to expand and develop your own professional expertise in the future.

Don't try to use the book all at once – that would feel like 'death by checklists' and would be demoralizing to say the least. Rather, we suggest that you select small areas of your practice to examine a little at a time, and use the checklists gradually, over a period of time.

Some ways to use this book

As a personal appraisal device

You can use this book entirely privately, to gather a detailed picture of the strengths you bring to your own teaching, and the areas where you wish to initiate changes or improvements as your work develops further.

As a team resource

For a group of colleagues working together, there's no need for every individual to be able to claim to meet each and every criterion in this book, but the more criteria that the whole team can claim to meet, the better will be the quality of the learning of the students you serve.

As an informal peer-feedback resource

You can select checklists where you would really like some independent feedback on your performance, and invite a trusted colleague whose opinions you value to complete the lists and talk you through the findings.

As a problem-identification resource

The checklists in this book will help individuals or teams of colleagues to diagnose areas which they may need to address specifically, to improve the overall quality of student learning.

As a framework for 'formal' appraisal

You can use these checklists while preparing for your appraisal, to achieve an accurate and detailed self-evaluation (in private). Those responsible for appraisal of teaching staff can also select checklists from this book to help them identify factors to consider in their appraisals.

As a 'teaching quality assessment' agenda

The checklists in this book are essentially addressed to the quality of *learning* – what better basis for 'teaching quality assessment'?

As a discussion-starter for staff development

We think this is probably the most productive use of our book. The checklists we have provided are only the start. Any group of dedicated colleagues can refine, extend and develop our lists to make more useful agendas for professional development.

As an instrument in preparing your portfolio

For example, if you are heading towards a teacher accreditation qualification (such as the scheme operated by the Staff and Educational Development Association (SEDA) in the United Kingdom), your analysis of your own practice using the grids will be a useful part of your evidence. The appendix gives details of how the SEDA scheme links to the topics covered in the grids.

Using the columns

For each of the checklist statements we have listed in this book, we have provided seven columns, and invite you to tick one or more as appropriate. We have added a further column for you to jot down action plan notes, or just keywords summarizing your own personal reactions to the statements. The column headings are:

I do this often This is simple, a chance for you to compile a profile of the many things you know you do well in your work already. These statements will help you to prepare evidence of your practice for appraisal and performance reviews.

I do this from time to time This too is a good answer. Many of the statements we have listed are not meant to be done all the time, but when appropriate.

I can do this when needed Who could ask more? This too is a valid answer.

I can't yet do this This may be really useful to you. It's always useful to know what we can't yet do, but may need to do sometime.

I'd like to be able to do this The statements where you tick this box can help you formulate your own personal and professional development targets, particularly while planning for the year ahead in reviews or appraisal.

I don't intend to do this A perfectly valid option! We can't do everything, even though it might be laudable to try!

I don't need to do this We believe you! In fact, it often helps to eliminate matters while building up a working agenda for the future.

Action plans or comments This column is of course too narrow for detailed plans. However, in our trialling of these grids, colleagues managed to insert phrases which could prove very useful to them in their further development and planning. Such comments included:

- Need to develop my competence here
- An area I'll concentrate on
- Something I've tried, will try more
- This will be hard for me!
- Important one
- Time is a problem here
- Essential that I do this
- Difficult because of wide audience.

Our 'piloteers' may have been too kind, of course, and it could sometimes be just as useful to write words in this column along the following lines:

- No way, not me
- I don't believe in this approach
- OK, give me 25 hours a day.

We've included a section at the end of the book (p134) to help you summarize what you may have gained from it, and to help you focus on the principal things you may plan to do as a result.

For the very brave only . . .

Some of these checklists *could* be completed by your students, to give you feedback about how they see your work in action. You could even invite them to include 'action plans or comments' for you.

Chapter 1

Teaching and Learning in Large Groups

Teaching quality seems to be directly associated with the things we do publicly, particularly our performance when dealing with large groups of learners. It is relatively easy for quality assessors to sit in during lectures, and to observe those parts of our work which focus on how we handle the one-to-many teaching–learning situation.

Working with large groups of learners is for many novices (and for many old hands too!) the most frightening and demanding part of our work. With large groups we are exposed, vulnerable, and dependent on our skills in the public performance domain. Furthermore, because large-group sessions are considered cost-effective, they are likely to seem to be the most significant part of our workload. Because we may be called 'lecturers' it would be damning if we were to be found lacking in the art of giving lectures! In recent years, we have been called upon to work with larger and larger numbers of students, usually with no increase in resources to help us. This is occurring just at a time when other pressures are being thrust upon us, such as the need to be actively involved in research and publication, and the requirement to adjust our curriculum to fit modular credit-rated schemes.

The fact is that most of the *real* learning which our students experience happens in all sorts of situations other than lecture theatres or large class-rooms. However, such is the tradition that we need to be seen to be able to give convincing performances in such places to be deemed competent teachers. This chapter provides a range of criteria which we may use to assess our skills and approaches to this side of our work.

We start with several checklists which deal essentially with **lecturing**, and in particular ways of making lectures interactive learning experiences for our learners. We include checklists about one of the most demanding aspects of lecturing – handling learners' questions. If we can get these parts of our work right, we are likely to be deemed competent teachers by quality assessors and appraisers.

In these checklists, we are not so much concentrating on the quality of the teaching performance, but on the quality of the learning which can be effected, even in very large group lectures. The secret is simple: not to concentrate on exposition as such, but rather to concentrate on getting the audience to think, make decisions, formulate questions, and *learn*.

We would like to emphasize that we are not anti-lecture as such; really good lectures can be powerful learning experiences. We all remember brilliant lecturers; indeed our own development may well have been influenced significantly by such individuals. We may have left such lectures inspired to learn more, and to give our best efforts in associated coursework or assignments.

However, we all remember not-so-brilliant lecturers too. In fact, most of us are not people with that special gift or aura to change our students' lives simply by the way we address them, certainly not *every* time we perform. That is why this chapter concentrates on things that any of us can do to help our students to learn.

Induction is a word found near the beginning of many a course timetable (and a new lecturer's programme too). Yet all too easily, induction (for staff and students alike) can seem an artificial rigmarole for which the relevance and purpose may only become apparent much later. We provide some checklist statements which aim to make student induction more valuable than this. Checklist criteria about the quality of induction may seem more relevant to Chapter 4, 'Helping learners individually', but we have included our thoughts on it here since many colleagues seem to be forever needing to induct larger numbers of students.

Also included in this chapter are some checklist questions about using **hardware**: if we make a mess of this, our performance may be downgraded by assessors or appraisers, and it is one of the key areas that students comment on when they complete evaluations. It is also an area where, if things go wrong, lecturers can lose confidence and students can become disruptive.

As with all the checklists in this book, we wish to remind you that we have absolutely no vision of the Perfect Teacher being able to claim 'I do this often' for each of the checklist statements! Such people do not exist.

For you as an individual, we invite you to use the checklists as a mapping device, to help you recognize which processes you already use to achieve successful learning for your students, and also to give you ideas of other approaches you may choose to experiment with as and when you find them appropriate or relevant to your own work.

1 Co-ordinating teaching with large groups

I develop appropriate administrative systems to keep effective records for large groups of learners, using the most appropriate technology available to me.

I plan that lecture programmes are built round learning-by-doing activities, rather than learners simply listening to my input.

I clarify and explain the links between lecture programmes and other elements of courses, such as practical work, projects, tutorials and seminars.

I plan to ensure 'equivalence of experience' when running parallel or repeated seminars or discussion groups.

I treat learners in large groups as individuals, for example by making sure that I know and use at least some of their names on each occasion.

I maintain regularly updated noticeboards (traditional or electronic) so that large groups of learners can keep abreast of course information and developments.

I facilitate opportunities to help members of large groups to get to know each other better, formally and informally.

I recognize and acknowledge the breadth of experience and knowledge that is already present in the learners themselves.

I make time available for learners in large groups to see me individually with queries or problems, for example by using an office-hours slot and a 'book your own appointment' process.

I ensure that feedback on assessed work done by large groups is sufficiently rapid to be of value.

I do this often	I do this from time to time	I can do this when needed	I can't yet do this	I'd like to be able to do this	I don't intend to do this	I don't need to do this	Action plans or comments

2 Lecturing to large groups

I prepare and publish in advance an outline of the aims and content of each lecture session.

I clarify the aims or objectives of each lecture at the start, explaining the intended learning outcomes associated with the lecture.

I check how many learners already have some experience of the topics, and use their experience when possible in the lecture.

I devise tasks and activities to be done during lectures, by learners both in buzz-groups, and individually.

I prepare clear briefings for the tasks which learners will do during each lecture, for example by making overhead transparencies of the tasks.

I gather from learners the products (for example on Post-Its) of their work on in-lecture tasks, for reports from buzz-groups, and explore matters arising.

I clarify assessment criteria relating to the topic of each lecture, and explain to learners what would be looked for in exam answers.

I put each lecture into perspective in 'the big picture', showing how each topic relates to those covered already, and those to come next.

I gather feedback from learners regularly in lectures, for example using short questionnaires, or Post-It exercises inviting learners to tell me what I should stop, start or continue doing.

I prepare handout materials which save learners having to copy down things they see and hear, and which contain activities and exercises.

I do this often	I do this from time to time	I can do this when needed	I can't yet do this	I'd like to be able to do this	I don't intend to do this	I don't need to do this	Action plans or comments

3 Asking rather than telling

In lectures, I pose questions and ask if anyone can suggest answers, rather than simply give learners information they may already know.

In small group sessions, I draw from learners everything they can tell me, rather than supplying information they may already know.

I give due credit and acknowledgement to learners who supply answers to questions I pose – including wrong answers! – while clarifying problematic areas.

I issue lists of questions for learners to consider and research, so that they can find out things in advance of lectures and tutorials.

In one-to-one consultations with learners, I find out what they already know, and give credit for this, before supplying information.

I ask learners to pinpoint their own questions, rather than assume I can guess what their questions are likely to be.

I turn things that learners need to know into questions to include in self-study learning materials for them to use at their own pace.

I remind learners that in due course they will be measured on the basis of their ability to answer questions, and encourage them to practise.

In small-group sessions with learners, I facilitate teams asking each other questions, and help judge their answers when needed.

I encourage learners to design assessment exercises and exam questions, to help them clarify what they need to become able to do.

I do this often	I do this from time to time	I can do this when needed	I can't yet do this	I'd like to be able to do this	I don't intend to do this	I don't need to do this	Action plans or comments

4 Providing a frame of reference for learners

I make use of aims, objectives, competence descriptors and statements of intended learning outcomes to let learners know what they are intended to achieve.

I keep a collection of learners' work from previous years, and use it in exercises to help learners identify the assessment criteria they face.

I help learners maintain a sensible balance regarding the amount of energy they devote both to my subject and to the overall course.

I discuss with learners typical past exam questions, and share the assessment criteria which were used to mark them.

Before learners undertake a coursework assignment which counts, I give them the chance to do a dummy run, perhaps using peer assessment for feedback.

In lectures, I help learners to understand the level of the evidence they should supply to demonstrate their knowledge.

In briefings for coursework assignments, I give clear details of the factors which will be considered in the assessment of the work.

In giving feedback on coursework, I give clear indications to learners regarding the appropriateness of the level of their work.

I facilitate groupwork where learners can openly discuss their views of the level of the work they may be expected to submit.

Where appropriate or possible, I negotiate standards with learners themselves.

I do this often	I do this from time to time	I can do this when needed	I can't yet do this	I'd like to be able to do this	I don't intend to do this	I don't need to do this	Action plans or comments

5 Handling questions from large groups (part 1)

I invite questions from learners in lectures, in such a way that it is easy and comfortable for them to ask questions.

I respond to spontaneous or invited questions in lectures, and deal with most of them successfully.

I admit when I do not know the answer to a question, and undertake to find it before the next session.

I give learners opportunities to write down questions for me during lectures (for example on Post-Its), so gathering questions from all learners, not just the least-shy ones.

I suggest that learners come to tutorials with lists of questions (individual or group lists) for fuller discussion at the tutorial.

I give learners the opportunity to answer each other's questions during lectures and tutorials.

I build in episodes of student question-setting as a group activity during some lectures (for example when I know that the topic is one where many learners will have questions to ask).

I bring in colleagues as expert witnesses to answer learners' questions, for example when there are some which I was unable to answer in the last session, or when an additional point of view will benefit learners.

I start lectures with a list of 'matters arising' questions or issues from the previous lecture, and go through this agenda before moving on to new material.

I ensure that learners who ask questions feel that their contributions are welcome and valued, not inconvenient.

I do this often	I do this from time to time	I can do this when needed	I can't yet do this	I'd like to be able to do this	I don't intend to do this	I don't need to do this	Action plans or comments

6 Handling questions from large groups (part 2)

I use techniques to ensure that question sessions are not monopolized by individuals.

I give learners opportunities to write down questions individually first, then select learners to ask them, or ask for volunteers to ask them.

I repeat each question to check that I've received it correctly and that everyone has heard it clearly.

When I am asked really important questions, I summarize them in writing on the overhead projector or board so that everyone can see exactly what I'm about to answer.

I arrange ways to deal with questions which could not be asked in class, for example by using a system of question cards and a question postbox.

I treat and deal with 'daft' questions as courteously as I do sensible ones.

I find out how many learners are keen to know the answer to important questions, and so help them to see how central such questions are for them.

When team-teaching with large groups, I arrange for colleagues to work with learners to help them formulate the most important questions to ask.

I arrange question-and-answer sessions where I am part of a panel with one or two colleagues, so that different answers can be compared by learners.

I check whether the learners who ask a question are satisfied with the answer received, and invite them to add any further comments of their own.

I do this often	I do this from time to time	I can do this when needed	I can't yet do this	I'd like to be able to do this	I don't intend to do this	I don't need to do this	Action plans or comments

7 Inducting students

I give new learners help and advice regarding finding their way about the building, the department, the campus and the local area.

I help new learners find out where relevant sources are in the library and other resource areas.

I alert learners to sources of information and advice about ways they can develop appropriate study skills.

I help learners locate staff and resources to help them develop or acquire word-processing and information technology skills.

I contribute to the provision of photographs of staff and students on noticeboards, to help learners to get to know each other, and to recognize staff.

In the first few lectures, I use discussion or buzz-group activities to help learners get to know each other.

In the first few seminar or tutorial sessions, I use fun games or simulations to help learners gain confidence and interact with each other.

I avoid swamping new learners with course documentation when they first arrive, and ensure that the papers I give them are directly relevant to their immediate needs.

I prepare and update regularly a course handbook, to help learners keep all the most useful information about the course in one place.

I alert new learners to the help available to them from support services, and I keep up to date with the names of the people they can consult about common problems or needs.

I do this often	I do this from time to time	I can do this when needed	I can't yet do this	I'd like to be able to do this	I don't intend to do this	I don't need to do this	Action plans or comments

8 Using the blackboard or markerboard

I remember to check with learners that my writing is large enough and easily legible.

I use the board to record key terms, phrases, diagrams and definitions, rather than for extended passages for learners to copy down.

I am careful about my use of coloured chalks or pens, recognizing the difficulty which many people experience seeing certain colours (for example red) from a distance.

I leave the board clear when my class is finished.

I ensure that learners have time to note down anything they need to from what I write on the board.

I provide handouts to support the information I write on the board, and to save learners from having to copy down large amounts of information.

I use the board to capture key words and ideas which I draw from the learners when I ask them questions.

In cases where showing a complete, complex diagram on an overhead transparency would make it difficult for learners to see its logic or structure, I use the board to draw up the diagram step-by-step, explaining as I draw.

I avoid speaking to the board, and wait till I have finished writing an item on it before turning to the class and talking about it.

I use the board for information which learners should keep in mind for extended periods in a lecture, for example while watching several consecutive overhead transparencies.

I do this often	I do this from time to time	I can do this when needed	I can't yet do this	I'd like to be able to do this	I don't intend to do this	I don't need to do this	Action plans or comments

9 Using overhead projectors

I am reasonably familiar with the operation of each of the types of overhead projector that I meet in the different classrooms and lecture rooms I use.

I adjust the position of the projector and screen so that all learners have a good view of my transparencies.

I ensure that the images fill the screen area, or a substantial area on a wall, so that learners at the back can still see the images clearly.

I adjust the focus and orientation of the projector, so that all parts of the image are in sharp focus.

I remember to switch off the projector when it is not needed (and bear in mind that the noise made by some projectors may interfere with my voice being heard by learners).

I point to particular parts of slides by using a pen or pencil on the slide itself, rather than gesticulating at the image on the screen.

I face the learners rather than the screen when discussing information displayed on the screen.

I take care not to remove slides before learners have finished reading them or making notes from them.

I continue unruffled when a bulb fails (or better still, can change the bulb myself, or switch to a spare bulb, or quickly acquire a new projector).

I write neatly on transparencies on-screen, for example when gathering learners' ideas from their buzz-group discussions in lectures.

I do this often	I do this from time to time	I can do this when needed	I can't yet do this	I'd like to be able to do this	I don't intend to do this	I don't need to do this	Action plans or comments

Chapter 2

Designing and Using Resources for Teaching and Learning

This chapter begins by looking in more detail at the design of **overhead transparencies** which may be used in large-group lectures. Teaching quality assessors will not fail to notice the quality of your overheads. If your slides are boring, congested and difficult to read the best lecture performance in the world will still be marred overall. If your slides are interesting, clear and attractive the worst lecture performance in the world may just be rescued! Also, it's worth remembering that the quality of teaching resources is frequently commented on by learners. Moreover, teaching resources such as overhead transparencies are also useful in small-group work, so it's worth our while paying attention to their quality and effectiveness.

If you need to be convinced, next time you are at a conference, note how audiences react to the quality of overheads. Watch the body language when people at the back can't read a slide. In fact, it's a worthwhile practice to sit at the back at conference presentations in general: we've found we sometimes learn a great deal about learning simply by observing the reactions of our fellow delegates.

Whereas overhead transparencies may be thought of primarily as teaching resources, **handout materials** are decidedly *learning* resource materials. Handout materials may be less spectacular than highly colourful or attention-grabbing overheads, but they are a more permanent indicator of the quality of teaching and learning that you set out to achieve. Quality assessors will probably get their hands on your handouts. In these times of readily available desktop publishing and advanced reprographics, it is perfectly possible for handout materials to look highly professional and attractive. However, it's not just how your handouts look that is important: it's what your handouts *do* for your learners that really matters.

Years ago, most student learning happened via notes taken in lectures. If one mastered all the lecture notes, an upper second class degree should be expected (to get a 'first' some evidence of wider reading was required). Nowadays, it's possible to replace much of the tedious business of students copying down what they see or hear in lectures; the main thrust of the lectures can be conveyed in the form of handouts. This can allow the actual lecture sessions to go into much more depth, analysing the meaning and significance of the handouts, rather than just 'delivering' the content. A much higher level of interaction between staff and learners is then possible.

Study guides are learning resource materials that learners can use to navigate their own way through the maze of published materials available in their subjects. Study guides can help learners to access a wide range of learning resources in libraries and resource centres. Such guides at their best can also help learners to check whether they are extracting the maximum learning payoff from the various learning materials they use. If we are honest with ourselves, most of the *real* learning that our students experience is likely to be derived from learning resource materials (books, journal articles, manuals, case-studies) and not from us directly. Perhaps the most we should expect of our part in the grand scheme of things is to pass on to our learners an enthusiasm to learn.

Open learning materials allow learners to learn in their own way, at their own pace, and under their own steam, and are probably the most powerful and versatile kind of learning resource materials being used now. Increasingly, open learning provision is not only offered as an alternative pathway to taught courses, but is included within such courses, where learners are given resource materials to learn suitable parts of the curriculum without formal teaching sessions.

We move next to **annotated bibliographies**. Have you noticed how much you can tell about the expertise of colleagues in your own field by seeing which books and references they rate most highly? We next address helping learners to use **libraries** or resource centres in general. Helping our learners to make the most of the resources available to them is a vital part of our work as teachers.

We conclude this chapter with two checklists addressing how we can use electronic media such as **e-mail, computer conferencing, multimedia** and **hypertext** to enhance our students' learning. When considering teaching quality, it does no harm at all to be seen to be selecting appropriately from a wide range of possible strategies and media, and with the growth in the attention and recognition given to the role of resource-based learning, it is satisfying to have at least a little of the high-tech end of the spectrum in our teaching portfolios as well as the overhead transparencies or chalk.

10 Preparing overhead projector transparencies

I am clear what purpose each transparency is to serve – whether an agenda for discussion, for information, illustration, to ask questions, humour, tasks, briefings, and so on.

I put a reasonable amount of text or information on each transparency – not crowded, not wasteful – using font sizes of 18pt or larger on laser-printed transparencies (24pt capital letters are approximately 6mm high).

I consider the visual impact of my transparencies, in terms of colour, layout and clarity of text, whether they are laser-printed or carefully hand-written.

I leave broad margins on all edges of a transparency, so that the content can fit easily into the area displayed by any projector ('square' design, A4 design, and so on).

I make it clear exactly what learners are intended to do with each transparency they see (copy it down, complete the unlabelled version in their handout, note it in passing, etc).

I work out carefully the best sequence in which to use transparencies in the context of particular lectures.

I label or number my transparencies so that they don't get out of order, and revise the numbering when I use them for different kinds of presentation.

I ensure that the language used on transparencies is clear and unambiguous, and appropriate for the context in which each is being used.

I use a system for keeping my transparencies in an organized way – for example a binder containing several plastic pockets each holding a set of related transparencies.

I remember to have with me some sheets of blank acetate, which I can overlay on pre-prepared transparencies to make ad-lib additions and amendments on any particular occasion.

I do this often	I do this from time to time	I can do this when needed	I can't yet do this	I'd like to be able to do this	I don't intend to do this	I don't need to do this	Action plans or comments

11 Using and designing transparencies

I check that all of my transparencies can be read easily at the back of the room, and refrain from using acetate photocopies from textbooks, documents or journals.

On handwritten transparencies, I use colours which can be read easily even in bright daylight (for example avoiding orange, yellow, and even red in large lecture theatres).

For printed overheads, I use desktop publishing formats which produce print much bigger and denser than a typewriter does.

I use visual images (cartoons, plans, line drawings) to add variety and interest to my presentations.

I employ sequential reveal (a bit at a time) of transparencies only when this is really useful, and I avoid learners feeling controlled in what they see and when.

I file my transparencies in the correct order before each lecture or presentation.

I use lower-case lettering (rather than UPPER-CASE) in any extended sentences or headings on transparencies to avoid eye-fatigue for learners.

I prepare ad hoc transparencies as appropriate during lectures, for example when responding to learners' questions or listing issues arising from discussions.

I use sheets of coloured acetate to make overhead slides, to add variety and interest to lectures and presentations.

I include the content of important overheads in learners' handouts, to avoid them having to waste time by copying down extended amounts of information during lectures.

I do this often	I do this from time to time	I can do this when needed	I can't yet do this	I'd like to be able to do this	I don't intend to do this	I don't need to do this	Action plans or comments

12 Designing handouts (part 1)

I use handout material to save learners having to copy down things I say.

I include in handout material information I show on overhead projector transparencies to save learners writing it all out again.

I include in handout material details of the expected learning outcomes associated with the topic of the handout.

I include in handout material annotated bibliographic details to help learners find the most useful sources of further information (see Checklist 16).

I prepare handouts well in advance of lectures, so that I don't put unnecessary pressure on reprographics services to supply them in good time.

I include in handouts practice exercises and activities, to allow learners to learn by doing, both in class-sessions and afterwards.

I make handout materials interactive, so that learners avoid switching off when they are given copies.

I ensure that handout materials contain space for learners to add their own comments, notes and questions as the session develops.

I compose handout materials on a word-processing system, so that the next edition can readily incorporate any feedback I receive on the present version.

I design handouts so that learners who are unable to be present for particular sessions can catch up on things they missed.

I do this often	I do this from time to time	I can do this when needed	I can't yet do this	I'd like to be able to do this	I don't intend to do this	I don't need to do this	Action plans or comments

13 Designing handouts (part 2)

My handouts are attractive in layout, using spacing and wording which make them readable and useful.

I am clear about the purposes of handout materials, such as whether they aim to provide wider reading, to give information, to give references, or to save learners writing notes during class sessions.

I ensure that the contents of my handouts are accurate, relevant, and up to date.

I make handouts available systematically to learners who miss the occasion when they are issued.

I design handout materials with clear directions for learners regarding what they should be doing with the subject material.

I number handouts clearly and systematically so learners can file them easily.

I avoid excessive use of large sections of unrelieved text in handouts.

I design handout materials so that they can be used for further learning, for example by including exercises and questions which learners can address as they study further.

I think 'green' regarding my production of handouts, so that I don't use large amounts of paper to produce handouts of little value to learners.

I make my handout materials available to colleagues, to help them see exactly what learners are studying in my own area of the subject.

I do this often	I do this from time to time	I can do this when needed	I can't yet do this	I'd like to be able to do this	I don't intend to do this	I don't need to do this	Action plans or comments

14 Assembling study guides

I identify suitable published resource materials, directly relevant to the content of my courses.

I decide which are the most important and relevant parts of published materials for learners to study.

I work out the intended learning outcomes or objectives that learners should become able to achieve after studying the texts.

I match the intended learning outcomes and objectives to the respective text materials, enabling learners to know what to study for each objective.

I write briefing notes, to help learners know exactly what they should be aiming to get out of studying each specified text.

I write learner-activities, so that learners can test themselves on the effectiveness of their studies as they use the texts.

I put together feedback responses, so that learners can estimate their success at attempting activities based on the texts.

I connect the intended outcomes, briefings, activities and feedback to make a support package for learners using the texts.

I test the validity and usefulness of the study guide material with pilot learners, and make adjustments as appropriate.

I explore the possibility of turning study guide material into a fully-developed self-study package for learners.

I do this often	I do this from time to time	I can do this when needed	I can't yet do this	I'd like to be able to do this	I don't intend to do this	I don't need to do this	Action plans or comments

15 Preparing open learning materials

I express the intended learning outcomes clearly, so that learners can see exactly what they are intended to achieve using open learning materials.

I illustrate the standard and depth of the intended learning outcomes, for example, by describing the sorts of evidence learners should accumulate to demonstrate their learning.

I build in plenty of learning-by-doing into the open learning materials, using self-assessment questions, exercises, and tutor-marked assignments.

I ensure that learners will derive useful feedback from the materials by providing feedback responses to self-assessment questions (not just the answers to the questions).

I check that learners' activities are closely matched to the intended learning outcomes of the materials.

I ensure that learners are allowed sufficient time to work through the materials (ie I don't expect them to do this on top of a full timetable).

I ensure that learners who encounter difficulties as they work through the materials have tutor backup.

I link assessed coursework to the content of the open learning materials, so that learners see how the topics covered by the materials fit into the total picture.

I gather feedback on the effectiveness of the materials, using questionnaires, and by discussing with learners any problems they encounter.

I update the materials regularly, to improve them on the basis of feedback gathered from learners, and on monitoring learners' performance in related assessments.

I do this often	I do this from time to time	I can do this when needed	I can't yet do this	I'd like to be able to do this	I don't intend to do this	I don't need to do this	Action plans or comments

16 Annotated bibliographies

I select carefully material to include in bibliographies, so that learners are not overwhelmed by the amount available to them.

I provide full details of all the items in my bibliographies so that learners can track down each item.

I provide comments about each source in a way that helps learners, rather than writing scholarly criticism to satisfy my own ego.

I include details to help learners know where to find the items in my bibliographies.

I regularly update my annotated bibliographies, and keep them on disk, so that a new issue can be given to learners at any time.

I prioritize items in bibliographies, so that learners can gain some idea of the relative importance of items.

I include a variety of sources, so that learners have some opportunity to follow their own interests and choose which sources they feel most comfortable with.

I ask learners for recommendations to add to annotated bibliographies, and show that I value their own knowledge and opinions.

I set learners group tasks to make their own annotated bibliographies on selected topics, then pool them with other groups and evaluate their usefulness.

I collect learners' own comments and reactions to important source materials, and include them (duly acknowledged) in my own bibliographies.

I do this often	I do this from time to time	I can do this when needed	I can't yet do this	I'd like to be able to do this	I don't intend to do this	I don't need to do this	Action plans or comments

17 Using libraries and information sources

I help learners to locate relevant information sources in the library and elsewhere.

I encourage learners to get to know the help and support they can gain from subject librarians.

I provide induction materials, workbooks and exercises to help my learners to learn to make use of the materials and resources in the library effectively.

I maintain good contacts with library staff, to help ensure that I am aware of the resources available, and am able to advise on future provision of resources.

I provide learners with appropriate practice exercises involving them developing their skills at identifying and locating relevant resource materials.

I ensure that when I provide bibliographies, I include only materials that are reasonably accessible to learners.

I set exercises which help learners to develop their skills at using citation indexes and databases available to them.

I give learners assignments and projects which require them to gain familiarity with the search facilities available to them through libraries.

I ensure that library staff are informed well in advance of the likely demand for particular books and journals.

I regularly suggest to library staff which new books and resources in my area are most worthy regarding purchase.

I do this often	I do this from time to time	I can do this when needed	I can't yet do this	I'd like to be able to do this	I don't intend to do this	I don't need to do this	Action plans or comments

18 Using e-mail and computer conferencing

I use electronic mail to communicate with colleagues in my own department and across my own institution.

I use electronic mail for academic and professional networking with colleagues in other institutions and countries (for example JANET, INTERNET, MAILBASE).

I use electronic mail to send individual feedback messages to learners, for example comments on their written work.

I use computer conferencing to provide noticeboard information directly to learners on my courses.

I encourage learners to use e-mail and computer conferencing to communicate with each other, and to develop their keyboard skills.

I make teaching resource materials such as handouts, assignments and exercises available to colleagues using e-mail and computer conferencing.

I log-on to the system at least once every day that I am on site, and reply to all e-mail messages straightaway.

I set learners tasks to perform by means of assessed contributions to computer conferences, for example book reviews or discussion papers.

I make the most of the merits of e-mail and computer conferencing, sending private comments to individuals by e-mail, and addressing common problems by entries to computer conferences.

I encourage learners to form self-help groups to enable them to get the most from electronic communication systems.

I do this often	I do this from time to time	I can do this when needed	I can't yet do this	I'd like to be able to do this	I don't intend to do this	I don't need to do this	Action plans or comments

19 Using multimedia and hypertext

I keep up to date with how I can use multimedia and hypertext software and hardware.

I work out how best multimedia and hypertext can supplement my students' learning.

I work out which areas of the curriculum particularly lend themselves to learning from multimedia and hypertext packages.

I experiment with designing my own multimedia or hypertext learning resource materials, and gather feedback from colleagues and from learners.

I experiment with the use of available authoring packages to develop well-structured learning materials.

I evaluate the merits and drawbacks associated with learning from multimedia and hypertext learning materials.

I check that the learning outcomes which can be achieved through commercially available multimedia or hypertext materials match the intended outcomes of my courses.

I explain to learners the exact nature of the learning outcomes they should derive from multimedia or hypertext materials, and explain what part these outcomes play in the overall course.

I evaluate the learning payoff associated with available learning packages, and select appropriate packages suited to the needs of my learners.

I collect feedback systematically from learners about their experience of using multimedia and hypertext learning resources, and act on the feedback to modify and improve the use of such resources.

I do this often	I do this from time to time	I can do this when needed	I can't yet do this	I'd like to be able to do this	I don't intend to do this	I don't need to do this	Action plans or comments

Chapter 3

Independent Study Tasks, Feedback, Groupwork and Assessment

This chapter brings together a range of overlapping themes central to effective learning. Learners learn much more from what they themselves *do* than from what we tell them or show them. Setting them appropriate tasks and exercises (including **independent study tasks**) is therefore central to successful learning. In this book we have already hinted strongly at the value of getting learners to *do* things even in the lecture situation. Here we go a stage further, and list some checklist criteria for the quality and effectiveness of tasks which learners can be asked to do on their own, or better still with their peers.

To feel positive about our achievements, we all need **feedback**. We need to know how we are doing. We need confirmation about the things we are doing well. We need to find out what to do about things we are not yet doing satisfactorily. Feedback to learners is probably the most crucial ingredient in any recipe for successful learning. In this chapter, we include checklists for both written feedback (for example our comments on essays, reports, assignments) and face-to-face feedback (for example in tutorials or tutor–student interviews).

Do you remember how much you learned from your fellow-students? For most of us, the real measure of our progress was how we found ourselves comparing to our peer group. We have therefore some checklists on **groupwork**. Perhaps the learning we derived from our fellow students was something that we controlled for ourselves, but it is perfectly feasible for such learning to be built in as part of the fabric of courses and learning programmes. Perhaps the most important step is to help learners to appreciate the **value** that they can derive from their colleagues.

In this chapter we go on to provide two checklists on the topic of **peer-assessment**. We have ourselves found that peer-assessment is one of the most powerful and effective ways of helping learners to learn deeply and successfully. Peer-assessment is not only a process which delivers to learners a great deal more feedback than they could receive from hard-pressed tutors; it is also a process which gives learners an understanding of the nature of the assessment criteria and standards which they may encounter in more formal forms of assessment such as exams. Peer-assessment, used well, empowers learners themselves, and gives them a strong sense of ownership of their learning.

While it is all very well to encourage learners to work in groups, and to devise tasks for them to do in groups, at some stage we are left with the matter of assessing how well the groupwork went. Our checklist on **assessing groupwork** aims to provide some ideas about how this difficult task may be approached.

Sooner or later, there always seems to be the formal exam. In this book we've said relatively little about exams (neither of us believes in them!) other than the suggestions contained in our checklist on **assessing large groups**. However, we have added a few pointers about **invigilating** them kindly!

20 Setting independent study tasks

I make it clear to learners how much time they should reasonably spend on my subject outside class-contact hours.

I give clear links between independent study tasks I set, and the intended learning outcomes or objectives learners are to achieve.

I suggest minimum and maximum amounts of time which would be reasonable to devote to each task I set.

I give word limits or other indicators to help learners gain a perspective of how much they should put into each task.

I ensure that learners receive task briefings clearly, eg by using printed sheets or overheads rather than giving an oral briefing.

I clarify how much (if at all) each assignment will count for in the overall scheme of assessment.

I give clear deadlines or cut-off dates by which each assessed task should be submitted.

I accommodate learners who for good reasons (sickness etc) fall behind schedule with assessed work.

I ensure that learners get feedback very rapidly on tasks they do (eg by giving out model answers when they submit their own work).

I help learners to see which learning objective each task addresses, and why it is useful for them to do it.

I do this often	I do this from time to time	I can do this when needed	I can't yet do this	I'd like to be able to do this	I don't intend to do this	I don't need to do this	Action plans or comments

21 Providing learners with written feedback

I avoid the use of red pens, because many learners associate red with criticism of an unconstructive nature.

I write legibly so students don't have to struggle to work out what I'm telling them.

I use assignment attachment sheets to avoid repetition as far as possible.

I use statement banks as appropriate, to allow me to provide each learner with more feedback than if I had to write it all out longhand.

I correct errors in work, but not to the extent of demoralizing learners.

I provide sufficient feedback so that learners get a realistic picture of how their work is going, and how they can improve it where necessary.

I provide opportunities for learners to discuss informally with me their reactions to written feedback.

I ask learners (either face-to-face or on feedback questionnaires) how useful or otherwise they are finding my written feedback comments.

I invite learners to indicate when handing in written work for marking what sorts of feedback they would particularly like to receive.

I keep copies of particularly important instances of written feedback to learners, so that I can quickly remind myself of exactly what was involved.

I do this often	I do this from time to time	I can do this when needed	I can't yet do this	I'd like to be able to do this	I don't intend to do this	I don't need to do this	Action plans or comments

22 Giving learners written feedback on marked work

I ensure that I include positive comments as well as any critical comments on each piece of work.

I let learners know of ways in which they can improve and develop on the basis of each piece of work.

I provide clues and references showing where learners can get more information to help them develop their work.

I give guidance on what to do next, so that learners continually have the opportunity to improve their work.

I give explanations for any acronyms or symbols used when marking learners' work.

I take care to ensure that my writing on learners' work is legible and that its meaning is clear.

I ensure that the feedback I give is purposeful and valuable rather than just critical.

I explain *why* things are wrong rather than just identifying things that are wrong.

I write phrases such as 'good point', 'I agree', 'definitely', 'quite so', 'this is the hub of the matter' rather than just putting ticks.

I ensure that I provide a response of some kind on every page of learners' work, even if very briefly.

I do this often	I do this from time to time	I can do this when needed	I can't yet do this	I'd like to be able to do this	I don't intend to do this	I don't need to do this	Action plans or comments

23 Giving learners face-to-face feedback

I make time to give learners feedback so that they don't feel rushed.

I usually start by saying something positive about the learner's work.

I avoid confrontational or hierarchical furniture patterns when I am sitting giving feedback (for example, I avoid sitting behind a high desk).

I watch learners carefully for cues so that I avoid overloading them with information.

I provide some kind of written backup for the more important things I say to learners.

I provide opportunities for learners to ask me questions, and encourage them to prepare questions to ask that will help them receive feedback.

I avoid patronizing learners, for example by finishing off their sentences for them when I know what they're going to tell me.

I ask learners to give me feedback about how they feel about my work with them.

When I have some particularly critical feedback to give, I offer learners the chance to say it for themselves, such as by asking 'What do you *really* think of that report?'

I ensure that each face-to-face feedback episode concludes on a positive note, and that learners leave with a smile where possible!

I do this often	I do this from time to time	I can do this when needed	I can't yet do this	I'd like to be able to do this	I don't intend to do this	I don't need to do this	Action plans or comments

24 Helping learners to value groupwork

I demonstrate to learners the benefits of working collaboratively with each other rather than always working competitively against each other.

I show learners the benefits gained by explaining things to each other – both by the 'explainer' and the 'learner'.

I encourage learners to work together in groups in lectures using appropriate tasks that can be done collaboratively even in a large-group situation.

I set groupwork tasks for learners in tutorless groups to undertake between lectures.

I help learners to form study syndicates, and to formulate groundrules for the successful operation of their syndicates.

I negotiate with learners the criteria for the assessment of the products of their groupwork, including details of how their respective contributions to the products may be estimated.

I facilitate the formation of groups of learners for specific tasks and activities, and use ways of rotating the group membership for different tasks, to promote cross-fertilization of ideas (and problems).

I suggest that learners keep a log of their groupwork activities, to form part of the evidence used to assess their groupwork.

I give examples of ways that I myself contribute to groupwork, and of the value I place on collaborative working.

I help learners working in groups to feel a sense of ownership of the operation of the group.

I do this often	I do this from time to time	I can do this when needed	I can't yet do this	I'd like to be able to do this	I don't intend to do this	I don't need to do this	Action plans or comments

25 Organizing groupwork

I identify parts of each syllabus that are best learned by students working collaboratively in groups.

I explain to students the aims of the work they are going to undertake in groups, and why the work is best approached in a collaborative way.

I write out briefings for groupwork tasks and issue the tasks to learners so that they can approach the work with clear targets in mind.

I explore the benefits of different group tasks going on in parallel, and students cross-fertilizing their products for the tasks.

When appropriate, I divide students into groups so that each group contains both high-fliers and low-fliers.

When appropriate, I structure groups on the basis of keenness and ability, so that the most able students can set higher standards for their work.

When appropriate, I allow students to self-select into groups, so that the ownership of each group resides with its members.

I help groups to formulate their own groundrules for the ways that members contribute to the work of the group.

I help groups to reflect on the processes of their groupwork, and to draw useful learning points from both successes and failures.

I assist groups to find times and places where they can work together in suitable surroundings and with useful resources.

I do this often	I do this from time to time	I can do this when needed	I can't yet do this	I'd like to be able to do this	I don't intend to do this	I don't need to do this	Action plans or comments

26 Organizing learners to peer-assess

I ensure that the criteria for assessment are clear, explicit, and understood by everyone who will apply them.

I provide opportunities for learners to formulate the criteria which they will later use in peer-assessment.

I give colleagues clear briefings on the operational management of student peer-assessment.

I provide learners (and colleagues) with a clear rationale explaining why peer-assessment is being used.

I provide learners with formative opportunities for the rehearsal of peer-assessment before they engage in peer-assessment events where the marks count.

I let learners' peer-assessment ratings count rather than moderating or over-ruling their assessments of each other's work.

I attempt to avert instances of over-assessment or under-assessment by excessively loyal or spiteful peers, by clarifying the nature of the assessment criteria and of the evidence which will be required.

I devise peer-assessment systems that are not excessively complex and are straightforward to implement.

I make full use of the opportunities for peer-feedback which accompany peer-assessment, and encourage debate and 'answering back'.

I offer to act as impartial troubleshooter should a difference of opinion emerge during peer-assessment.

I do this often	I do this from time to time	I can do this when needed	I can't yet do this	I'd like to be able to do this	I don't intend to do this	I don't need to do this	Action plans or comments

27 Organizing learners in peer-assessment

I demonstrate to learners the value of peer-assessing as a deep-learning device.

I give learners practice at devising assessment criteria, and applying the criteria to examples of past students' work.

I use peer-assessment in a variety of contexts, for example essays, reports, posters, laboratory work, presentations, and tests.

I help learners to identify useful assessment criteria for tasks they are about to undertake.

I help learners to devise weightings for their assessment criteria, reflecting the relative importance of each assessment element.

I help learners to clarify the nature of the evidence which will be suitable to demonstrate the achievement of particular criteria.

I produce grids of the criteria and weightings decided by learners, to enable them to record their peer-assessment data.

I facilitate learners' peer-assessing, with them recording their data into grids.

I participate with learners in their peer-assessment, confirming that the average of their assessments is similar to that which I would give with shared, known criteria.

I analyse learners' peer-assessment data efficiently, working out their average peer-assessment rating for each performance.

I do this often	I do this from time to time	I can do this when needed	I can't yet do this	I'd like to be able to do this	I don't intend to do this	I don't need to do this	Action plans or comments

28 Assessing groupwork

I include assessed groupwork in my courses alongside other more traditional forms of assessment.

I help learners to work out what sort of evidence they will need to furnish for the work of their groups.

I help learners to understand what the performance criteria will be for the assessment of their groupwork.

I encourage learners to explore how they can make different, but equally valid, contributions to the work of the group.

I help learners face up to their responsibility regarding any problems due to passengers in group work.

I help learners to distinguish between the assessment of the product of the group, and that of their individual contributions.

When appropriate, I use assessed groupwork tasks to develop group skills rather than as an assessment device as such.

If a dispute arises in a group regarding an individual's contribution, I facilitate discussions to resolve the issue rather than dictate a solution.

I am willing to consider alternative means of assessment in occasional circumstances where a particular learner cannot participate adequately in a group for good reasons.

I help learners to identify the particular competences and skills upon which successful groupwork depends.

I do this often	I do this from time to time	I can do this when needed	I can't yet do this	I'd like to be able to do this	I don't intend to do this	I don't need to do this	Action plans or comments

29 Assessing large groups

I clarify the nature of the assessment criteria to be employed in formal assessments, so that learners can prepare appropriately for assessment.

I make the purposes of each assessment clear, for example whether the primary intention is for learners to gain feedback, or whether the assessment is summative.

When tutor-assessing the work of large groups of learners, I issue model-answers, or commentaries, so that learners receive immediate feedback on their efforts.

As soon as a large group of learners have submitted work for tutor-assessment, I issue the assessment criteria I am going to use, allowing them to begin to self-assess their attempts at once.

When formulating assessment criteria for large-group assessment, I gain feedback from colleagues on the appropriateness of my choices of criteria.

When setting examination questions, I seek feedback from colleagues on the clarity of my wording for each question, and the standards of the questions.

Wherever possible, I maximize the feedback that large groups of learners receive on assessed coursework, by preparing handouts containing specimen answers and discussion commentaries.

I help learners in large groups to understand the nature of formal assessment, for example by using some lectures to guide them through the assessment of selected past answers.

After formal examinations, I write a feedback report for learners (and future learners) indicating common problems encountered by candidates.

Where possible, I discuss with individual learners their own performance in formal assessments, and give them as much feedback as I can to help their future learning.

I do this often	I do this from time to time	I can do this when needed	I can't yet do this	I'd like to be able to do this	I don't intend to do this	I don't need to do this	Action plans or comments

30 Invigilating fairly and kindly

I am watchful of learners' needs, ensuring they do not run out of paper or other resources.

I ensure that examinations start and finish promptly, and that learners have all they need for the exam before they begin to write their answers.

I avoid intimidating candidates by being as unobtrusive as possible as I undertake the task.

I ensure that clocks in the exam room are working and visible, and I give at least two time-reminders towards the close of the exam.

I am aware of the ways in which cheating may be attempted, and I try to prevent it from starting rather than have to confront it when it happens.

I am vigilant to detect any cheating, and quick to take action if I detect it (but without causing disturbance to the rest of the candidates).

I have contingency plans for emergencies, and know how to get help when necessary.

I deal promptly and reassuringly with any problems learners bring to my attention in exams.

Where the colleague who set a question needs to be contacted for clarification or explanation, I suggest that anyone who is stuck on that question should focus their attention on other parts of the paper meanwhile.

If an obviously anxious or stressed candidate catches my eye, I smile reassuringly.

I do this often	I do this from time to time	I can do this when needed	I can't yet do this	I'd like to be able to do this	I don't intend to do this	I don't need to do this	Action plans or comments

Chapter 4

Helping Learners Individually

When it comes to formally assessing or appraising the quality of our teaching, the most important things may well be left out altogether, as they are difficult to measure, and often essentially quite private. In this chapter we have collected together a number of aspects of effective teaching which are not really teaching as such, rather being supportive and helpful to individual learners. These aspects of our work may be much less public than our skills at giving lectures or designing learning resource materials, but to individual learners it is often the way we handle the themes included in this chapter that matters most.

With growing numbers of students, it gets harder for us to know them by **name**. Yet to students themselves, it makes a big difference if they feel they are not just lost in a crowd, but individuals known by their teachers.

Most universities and colleges operate some sort of **personal tutoring** system, but relatively few such systems actually work nearly as well as may be intended! We list some criteria which aim to make personal tutoring much more significant and effective than is the norm in our experience.

With increased numbers of learners on many courses, the chance to deal with questions and problems of individual learners is under some threat. **Being available** becomes more of a challenge; we offer in our checklist some food for thought about how this may be achieved.

We have also included a checklist addressing the particular needs of **overseas students** as they sometimes need rather more individual attention than the average learner. Indeed, overseas learners often feel particularly *individual*, and their particular problems and anxieties may well sometimes be unique.

Problem solving is a skill needed throughout anyone's career and life, our own as well as those of our students. Helping learners to develop problem-solving skills is one of the most valuable things we can do for them as individuals, and we have therefore included in this chapter some checklist criteria relating to this area of our work.

Student projects are often vitally important, particularly towards the final stages of their courses. For many students, the quality of the direction and supervision they receive during their project work is crucial, and therefore we feel it is important to suggest some criteria for the quality of such supervision. Student projects can be a valuable learning-by-doing experience, and can provide vital preparation for progression to research for those learners aiming for higher degrees. With more students and projects to supervise, we hope that the criteria in our checklist will help colleagues to focus their efforts in this task more productively.

Earlier in this book, we pointed out the value of helping students to learn from each other. **Proctoring** (experienced students supporting the learning of less-experienced students) is a way of capitalizing on the benefits of peer-group teaching and learning. It is worth remembering that the most significant learning payoff of proctoring is often a deeper understanding of subjects by the proctors themselves as they explain things to their less-experienced colleagues. It's also worth us reminding ourselves that someone who has only recently learned something can often explain it more successfully than someone who has known it for years (the former person remembers what it felt like to see the light dawn).

As the trend continues to help learners to develop greater ownership of their learning, the benefits of **negotiating learning agreements** become more important and powerful. Our checklist on this lists the key stages for maintaining standards in such agreements while at the same time providing flexibility. Particularly crucial is the clarity of the intended outcomes of learning agreements, and the nature of the evidence which learners will aim to assemble to demonstrate their accomplishments.

Many of our learners will require **references** as they apply for employment or move further in their education. This is essentially a somewhat private and intimate part of our professional work, but some checklist criteria may be helpful in developing our consciousness of the importance of this aspect of our work.

31 Getting to know learners' names

I encourage learners to get to know each other's names, and to use them in sessions (including large-group lectures).

I remember how insulting it is to get someone's name wrong or even to spell it wrongly on a class list or notice, and ensure that I don't.

I provide learners with opportunities to write their own names, for example on badges, place-cards, or even Post-Its in large-group sessions (they know how to spell them correctly).

I don't base my data on learners' names entirely on departmental lists, but build my own list including forenames rather than initials.

I accept that learners may want to be called by something other than their official names, and ask them to tell me what they would prefer.

I use games, rounds, and memory-aids to help me learn the names in a group and to help the learners remember each other's names.

Whenever I can, I address each learner by name, and check that I am doing so accurately.

I make it clear what I prefer learners to call me, and in what circumstances I am happy to be called by my own first name.

I take care not to embarrass learners whose names are difficult for me to pronounce, and practise till I can use their names as easily as those of their colleagues.

I am careful to use colleagues' names sensitively (for example to check whether Archie really prefers to be referred to as Dr Podworthy).

I do this often	I do this from time to time	I can do this when needed	I can't yet do this	I'd like to be able to do this	I don't intend to do this	I don't need to do this	Action plans or comments

32 Being a personal tutor (part 1)

I have a system whereby I identify the learners for whom I am personal tutor within a week or so of them starting their courses.

I am able to learn who my tutees are relatively quickly, for example from a set of photographs.

I make sure that the learners for whom I am personal tutor feel welcome and part of the University soon after their arrival on campus.

I share my attention equally among personal tutees, without regard to any personal preferences on my part.

I make clear distinctions between my role as personal tutor and the roles of other people such as counsellors, academic tutors and other advisors.

I make efforts to keep the contact names and telephone numbers of those who can help when I cannot, such as counsellors, chaplains, accommodation officer, health centre.

I ensure that I undertake all my duties with tutees taking equal-opportunities principles into account.

I am sensitive and receptive to the individual needs of the learners for whom I am personal tutor.

I choose neutral territory (for example, a coffee bar) for interviews with personal tutees which could include critical feedback to them.

I establish contacts with colleagues to ensure that I am updated regularly with the performance and progress of the learners for whom I am personal tutor.

I do this often	I do this from time to time	I can do this when needed	I can't yet do this	I'd like to be able to do this	I don't intend to do this	I don't need to do this	Action plans or comments

33 Being a personal tutor (part 2)

I set aside time each week for personal tutoring activities, rather than regard it as something to be done only when the need arises.

I consider carefully the physical setting where I give tutorials, paying due regard to learners' comfort and security.

I arrange an introductory meeting with each tutee, in which we make shared notes of the main aims and requirements of each tutee.

I actively follow the progress of each tutee, consulting colleagues to find out if there are any difficulties where I may need to help.

I strike a reasonable balance regarding the boundaries of my role as personal tutor.

I ask each tutee to keep me up to date with changes of address (or courses), and keep an up-to-date record of their circumstances.

I offer to undertake an 'honest broker' role in any difficulties my tutees have with their courses or lecturers.

I proactively seek out those tutees whose progress I find is 'at risk' in discussions with colleagues.

I maintain contact with counsellors and others whose help may sometimes be needed, and don't pretend to have answers to all problems.

At assessment boards, I ensure that I am briefed to be able to speak on behalf of each of my tutees if the need arises.

I do this often	I do this from time to time	I can do this when needed	I can't yet do this	I'd like to be able to do this	I don't intend to do this	I don't need to do this	Action plans or comments

34 Being available to learners

I confirm to learners that I am ready to see them individually or in groups, about any appropriate issues they want to consult me on.

I advertise through the departmental office particular times of the week when I will be available to see learners by appointment.

I encourage learners to write questions or comments, and give or send them to me, so I can prepare replies for them.

I allow time at the end of lectures and other teaching sessions for learners to approach me for advice or to ask questions.

I clarify to learners the particular sorts of questions and enquiries I am most ready to discuss with them.

I ensure that learners who seek me out for advice or to ask questions do not feel intimidated or unwelcome.

I suggest that learners in groups work out agendas of issues they would like me to discuss, or questions they would like to pose.

I ensure that meetings by prior arrangement with learners are not unnecessarily cancelled or interrupted.

I keep records of interactions with learners, so I can inform the rest of the class of advice which may be needed, or of decisions taken.

I arrange for a colleague to handle questions on my behalf if I am not available at a previously advertised time.

I do this often	I do this from time to time	I can do this when needed	I can't yet do this	I'd like to be able to do this	I don't intend to do this	I don't need to do this	Action plans or comments

35 Working with learners from overseas

I give informed advice to overseas learners about my institution's admission regulations.

I give informed advice to overseas learners about financial matters that are likely to be particularly important to them.

I am able to advise overseas learners where to go for further help and information, for example Student Services, the International Office, British Council, and so on.

I give particular support when necessary to overseas learners regarding the development of their study skills to meet the assessment requirements they will encounter.

I am actively involved in the induction of overseas learners, helping them to familiarize themselves with the context and ethos of my institution.

When I design learning resources such as handout materials, I ensure that the language I use does not place additional barriers before overseas learners.

In small group sessions, I ensure that overseas learners are given adequate time to air any particular problems that they may be experiencing.

I make it my business to become more acquainted with the culture and background of typical overseas learners in my classes.

When setting assignment tasks and assessment questions, I ensure that overseas learners are not disadvantaged by the language I use in my questions or instructions.

I ensure that overseas learners feel that they can approach me for clarification or explanation when they feel they need it.

I do this often	I do this from time to time	I can do this when needed	I can't yet do this	I'd like to be able to do this	I don't intend to do this	I don't need to do this	Action plans or comments

36 Helping learners to solve problems

I help learners to put problems in perspective and to retain a sense of proportion.

I make time to see learners with problems, and accept that a problem that seems simple to me can at the time seem like an enormous obstacle to them.

I encourage learners to identify exactly what their problems are, as a necessary preliminary to finding practical solutions to them.

I help learners to establish whose problems they really are – reminding them that only the owner of a problem can expect to solve it.

I suggest to learners that they undertake an exercise on how to make a problem worse, as a means of identifying possibilities for improving things.

I listen to learners as they explain their problems, and avoid taking any stance which may be construed as judgemental.

When I don't know what to do about learners' problems, I try to find someone with the necessary experience to help.

I help learners to regard problems as positive learning opportunities, and as chances to acquire new skills and competences.

I put learners at ease regarding approaching me with their problems, and open up channels of communication.

When appropriate, I suggest that peer-group help can be valuable regarding problem-solving, and suggest ways of seeking such help.

I do this often	I do this from time to time	I can do this when needed	I can't yet do this	I'd like to be able to do this	I don't intend to do this	I don't need to do this	Action plans or comments

37 Supervising projects

I make it clear to learners how much their projects count for in the overall context of their courses.

I help learners to plan the intended outcomes of their individual projects, and give feedback on the appropriateness of the level of these outcomes.

I help learners to ensure that their planned project work is relevant to their courses, and that the scope and range of the work they plan is realistic.

I help learners to decide on staged deadlines for their project work, and to arrange meetings or interviews so they can check their progress.

I provide learners with examples of work done for past projects, so they can adjust their own aims and targets appropriately.

I help learners to work out the nature of the criteria which will be used to assess their project work, and clarify the standards they should aim to meet.

I encourage learners to discuss their project work with each other, to gain feedback on their progress.

I provide or organize advice and counselling for those learners who have serious difficulties with their project work.

When assessing project work, I provide feedback which will help learners address project work which they may encounter later in their courses.

I allow extra time to learners who, for genuinely unforeseen causes, fall behind in their project work.

I do this often	I do this from time to time	I can do this when needed	I can't yet do this	I'd like to be able to do this	I don't intend to do this	I don't need to do this	Action plans or comments

38 Setting up proctoring

I give the proctors credit for their work (for example by including a reflective log of their proctoring work as part of their assessed coursework in its own right).

I explain that the act of explaining something to someone who does not yet understand it is one of the best ways to deepen the explainer's own understanding of it.

I remind learners that someone who has recently learned something can often explain it better than someone who has known it for a long time (and forgotten how it was learned).

I ensure that learners don't consider that proctoring is a cop-out by their teaching staff, but is a complementary part of their learning.

I set up mechanisms for the supported learners to evaluate the effectiveness of their learning from their proctors (to help them reflect and deepen their learning).

I provide a range of useful learning resources (handouts, videos, references to the literature) to proctors, on which they can design their own 'teaching' strategies.

I establish whole-group events, at which any problems encountered by proctors or learners can be aired and resolved.

I ensure that the learning outcomes of those topics that are to be learned from proctors are clearly expressed, so that both proctors and learners know when successful learning has taken place.

I provide backup mechanisms so that when particular difficulties arise, alternative help is available without anyone losing face or self-esteem.

I supply self-assessment tests to learners, to help them ascertain whether or not their learning from their proctors has been successful.

I do this often	I do this from time to time	I can do this when needed	I can't yet do this	I'd like to be able to do this	I don't intend to do this	I don't need to do this	Action plans or comments

39 Negotiating learning agreements

I identify parts of the curriculum where it is appropriate for learners to have some choice over what they learn, and at what pace.

I select areas of the curriculum which allow learners to choose how they prefer their learning to be assessed, and at what time.

I help learners to formulate or select their learning objectives or intended learning outcomes, providing specimen outcomes to assist them in finding an appropriate level.

I help learners to work out details of the evidence they should accumulate to demonstrate their achievement of their chosen objectives.

I encourage learners to choose their own timescales for the work they will do as part of their learning agreements.

I provide skeleton proformas and examples of completed agreements, so that learners can draw up their own particular learning agreements.

I negotiate with learners as necessary, to ensure that their learning agreements are of an appropriate standard and level, trying to leave learners with as much ownership of their plans as possible.

I ensure that each learner has a signed, dated copy of the agreement, and that I keep a copy.

I encourage learners to renegotiate their learning agreements whenever necessary, rather than fall behind schedule and give up working towards the agreements.

I help learners build into their learning agreements review times and dates, so that timescales and targets can be adjusted on an ongoing basis.

I do this often	I do this from time to time	I can do this when needed	I can't yet do this	I'd like to be able to do this	I don't intend to do this	I don't need to do this	Action plans or comments

40 Giving references for further study and employment

I make it clear to learners that I am willing to provide references on their behalf to employers or other colleges.

I make sure that learners know that I will give fair references, and will not extol their virtues if they are lazy or antisocial!

I explain to learners what they must do to get the most out of me as a referee (for example keeping me informed of who may contact me for references).

I keep 'mugshot' photographs in my files for each learner, so I can remember exactly who each one is.

I keep organized records of the work and performance of learners, so I can draw on them later when providing references.

I customize standard references to make them appropriate for individual learners in specific contexts.

I carefully check my information to ensure that what I say about each learner is accurate.

I explain to learners that I am willing to give them a good idea of what I will have to say about them in a reference.

When appropriate, I provide learners with a copy of what I have said about them (for example to boost their confidence, or help them prepare for interview).

I suggest that learners should write down what they would really like to be said about them in a reference, as a self-analysis and developmental activity.

I do this often	I do this from time to time	I can do this when needed	I can't yet do this	I'd like to be able to do this	I don't intend to do this	I don't need to do this	Action plans or comments

Chapter 5

Personal and Professional Qualities and Skills

This in some ways is a rounding-off chapter, addressing a range of areas in which we need to be competent professional people. That said, the topics we have chosen to cover under this umbrella title are probably more important than anything else we have addressed elsewhere in this book; indeed this chapter is the longest, and the broadest.

The first four checklists are essentially intended to help us to measure our **interactive skills**, both with our own colleagues, and with the other people we need to work with. Sometimes it's not easy to get on with everyone: we don't claim to be easy to get on with ourselves! We have therefore included a couple of checklists of criteria for coping with difficult people (and we only wish we could claim to meet each of the criteria we have listed!).

Record-keeping, though important, is all too easily neglected. We hope that our checklist on this will help alert colleagues to some of the things that can be done to improve this.

Equal opportunities addresses a cluster of dimensions that is more important than any other issue included in this book. It would take another volume to address this properly, but we hope that our list of checklist statements helps you to self-assess the extent to which your own professional work demonstrably upholds the principles of equal opportunity.

The final five checklists in our book are essentially about **self-appraisal** and **self-evaluation**. It is important that we continue to learn, and especially important that we continue to learn about learning! We know a very distinguished colleague who continues to learn about learning by enrolling as a learner on some programmes offered by his own institution.

It is always useful for us to rejoice in our **strengths**, and even more useful (if less pleasant) to analyse our **weaknesses**. This book is intended to help with both. Every time you can confidently tick the 'I do this often' column, you have identified a strength in your work. The column 'I'd like to be able to do this' is, if you like, the weakness column – but our real weaknesses are the ones we don't yet know about, not the ones we're aware of.

With increased pressures on us to be both excellent teachers and respected researchers at the same time, we need to take stock of our own **scholarship**. Scholarship is a difficult subject to pin down – try asking 20 colleagues to define it in a couple of sentences! We hope that our checklist on this is helpful and practical.

With **appraisal** interviews becoming the norm in the life of academics (as they have been for many years in several other walks of life), a checklist focusing on the sorts of preparation that we can make for such interviews should be of value. Our final checklist looks at **planning for future development** and again should be a valuable agenda to use when preparing for appraisal interviews. In the final analysis, however, whatever we meet in our encounters with quality assessors or appraisers, the views of two categories of people count more than anything else: our learners and ourselves. *They* know what we're really like; *we* need to be self-aware as objectively as we can.

Finally we provide a short self-analysis questionnaire to enable you to summarize and clarify what you have gained from the whole of this book.

We hope that this book helps colleagues to find out more about themselves and their work, and that it gives much more comfort than anxiety. In a way, we would like to think that it constitutes a framework which helps colleagues to contemplate the nature and direction of their own future professional and personal development. The act of writing the checklists has caused us to contemplate our own development needs in some depth! Anyone with no development needs is one of two things: perfect – or past it!

As we said at the outset, it is not our aim to delineate a model of teaching *perfection*. Rather, we have provided an agenda to serve as a basis for individuals addressing particular facets of their work, with a view to achieving our common goal of enhancing the quality of learning our students achieve.

41 Team teaching

We co-produce teaching and learning materials as much as possible to produce co-ownership of resources.

We brief colleagues working with us carefully, especially part-time colleagues or service lecturers who could not be with us during planning discussions.

We plan and organize our work well in advance, for example, using flow-charts to show how our roles will integrate.

We keep each other informed of what we are doing and how it is going.

We provide emergency backup for each other to cope with contingencies.

We provide social opportunities for each other, so we can enjoy each other's company out of the context of our work.

We ensure that when our views or opinions differ, we avoid arguing in the presence of learners!

We promote the benefits of team teaching to colleagues, and help them start to work in teams.

We take opportunities to learn from each other's specialist knowledge and skills, and to learn to be able to do each other's work as necessary.

We take time to review openly the processes by which we work together, and improve and develop them whenever we can.

I do this often	I do this from time to time	I can do this when needed	I can't yet do this	I'd like to be able to do this	I don't intend to do this	I don't need to do this	Action plans or comments

42 Being a good collaborative colleague

I meet deadlines for collaborative tasks when colleagues are relying on me keeping to schedules.

I am punctual when attending meetings and ensure that I have prepared properly for them.

I keep my colleagues briefed about what I'm currently working on.

I avoid presenting colleagues with urgent tasks at the last minute.

I make contingency plans with colleagues to cover emergencies when the unexpected may prevent them (or me) from working as normal.

I am generous with my time, effort and energy as far as is compatible with my own priorities.

I make available to colleagues my teaching materials, including over-heads, handouts, and exercises.

I invite colleagues to observe or participate in some of my sessions with learners, and ask for their comments about how the sessions went.

I respond to colleagues' invitations or requests to sit in on their sessions, and give them feedback tactfully and supportively when they request it.

I seek advice and suggestions from colleagues (even when I don't need it) and make them feel valued and respected for their help.

I do this often	I do this from time to time	I can do this when needed	I can't yet do this	I'd like to be able to do this	I don't intend to do this	I don't need to do this	Action plans or comments

43 Mentoring new colleagues

I provide an environment in which new colleagues feel supported and welcomed.

I make it easy for new colleagues to ask me questions.

I provide *written* briefings on key issues for new colleagues covering both formal and informal matters.

I am supportive and helpful regarding informal matters such as coffee clubs, social facilities and photocopier arrangements.

I provide oral briefings for new colleagues before they attend formal meetings to help them understand the context and background of the meetings.

I ensure that new colleagues are quickly brought into information chains, mailing lists and administrative systems.

I make time to introduce new colleagues personally to other staff whom I suggest they talk to, rather than simply sending them along.

I encourage new colleagues to sit in on my own work and to work with me as they gain confidence and experience.

When I can not help with a problem brought to me by a new colleague, I seek out a person who can help rather than just suggesting a name.

I create informal time with new colleagues, such as lunches out and evening get-togethers, and build up a relationship where they feel they can approach me for any help they need.

I do this often	I do this from time to time	I can do this when needed	I can't yet do this	I'd like to be able to do this	I don't intend to do this	I don't need to do this	Action plans or comments

44 Valuing support staff

I regard my time as no more important than anyone else's.

I recognize that poor planning on my part should not result in excessive urgency of deadlines for other people.

I brief colleagues in advance whenever I think there may be heavy workloads coming up for them.

I recognize that other people have hectic periods in their work and lives, and don't take their time or help for granted.

I don't scapegoat part-time staff when they leave work at the end of their required period of duty.

I clear up my own mess, for example flipcharts, coffee-cups, Post-Its, table and chair arrangements.

I take my turn at shopping for and making the tea and coffee.

I clarify which jobs are really urgent, and try to give support colleagues work that is not urgent whenever possible.

I acknowledge the help of support staff (for example in publications, handout materials, reports to committees and so on).

I ensure that learners regard support staff as professional people, and not as people they can exploit or disregard.

I do this often	I do this from time to time	I can do this when needed	I can't yet do this	I'd like to be able to do this	I don't intend to do this	I don't need to do this	Action plans or comments

45 Contributing effectively to meetings

I file committee papers systematically, so that I always have an up-to-date record of the work of each committee I am involved with.

Before each committee meeting, I read the minutes of the previous meeting, and jot down 'matters arising' that I consider should be addressed.

I ensure that when I have been given a task to undertake at a previous meeting, I am in a position to report my progress at the next meeting.

When I am critical of a point of view adopted by other members of a committee, I ensure that I have positive suggestions to give regarding the action that could be taken.

When I offer critical comments, I do so in a way that does not criticize other people, but addresses weaknesses I see in particular policies and actions.

When I have raised a point at a meeting, I offer to research the issue concerned before the next meeting, and supply a paper to be discussed at that meeting.

I subscribe to the philosophy of 'executive committees' where each member has an area of responsibility, and there are no passengers.

When serving as secretary to a committee, I ensure that the minutes of meetings are circulated very promptly, and that each meeting has a clearly spelled-out agenda.

When acting as chair of a committee, I try to ensure that each member has equal opportunity of presenting views and opinions.

I ensure that when expressing my own views at a committee meeting, I concentrate on issues and policies, rather than allow personal differences with other members to surface.

I do this often	I do this from time to time	I can do this when needed	I can't yet do this	I'd like to be able to do this	I don't intend to do this	I don't need to do this	Action plans or comments

46 Coping with difficult people
(if you achieve all of these you are either a saint or an angel – tell us how you do it!)

I maintain a professional stance when others are being petty, bureaucratic, or conflictual.

I have appropriate coping strategies which enable me to handle other people's unprofessional behaviour (for example, temper tantrums, personal aggression).

I manage to avoid the temptation to use improper channels (gossiping, bitchiness, etc) when faced with difficult colleagues.

I recognize occasions when I myself am being difficult, and admit it or apologize for it.

I endeavour to perceive difficulties in terms of actions or situations, rather than in terms of people.

I avoid difficulties encountered with people in one situation spilling over into different situations involving the same people.

I make the first move to 'rebuild bridges' when I have experienced difficulties with people.

I rehearse what I'd like to tell difficult people along the lines of what I would like them to do differently, rather than resorting to insulting behaviour.

I use encounters with difficult people to learn more about myself, and to improve my abilities to handle adversity.

I try to find out the circumstances which may lead to people behaving in a 'difficult' way, and to understand their point of view even when I cannot agree with it.

I do this often	I do this from time to time	I can do this when needed	I can't yet do this	I'd like to be able to do this	I don't intend to do this	I don't need to do this	Action plans or comments

47 Dealing with difficult colleagues

I distinguish carefully between conflicts of ideas and conflicts of personality.

I refrain from inappropriately aggressive behaviour in conflict situations, including temper tantrums, shouting, storming out, indulging in sarcasm or cynical comments.

I suspend judgement and listen to others' views in discussions and in other contexts.

I do not let previous conflicts or differences of opinion colour current interactions.

I provide a safe environment for teaching, learning and interaction with colleagues, where conflict is minimized, and managed sensitively should it arise.

I think before I speak, and listen before I respond to others.

I value others' opinions, and respect their right to hold them, even when diametrically opposed to my own views.

When I know I have been unnecessarily difficult, I set an example by apologizing, and admitting that I acted unreasonably or thoughtlessly.

I look on encounters with difficult colleagues as useful learning experiences for me, to help me improve the ways I interact with people in conflict situations.

I avoid temptations and opportunities to undermine the professional dignity or self-esteem of colleagues whose behaviour has been inappropriate or negative.

I do this often	I do this from time to time	I can do this when needed	I can't yet do this	I'd like to be able to do this	I don't intend to do this	I don't need to do this	Action plans or comments

48 Ensuring effective communication with learners

I ensure that learners are aware of the location of relevant noticeboards for course information.

I make sure that noticeboard information concerning my courses is regularly updated, and well set out.

I contribute to departmental student newsletters, or other circulars to keep learners informed about course developments.

I ensure that learners are aware of the times and places at which I am available for individual consultation.

I maintain updated records of my learners' addresses, e-mail addresses and (where possible) telephone numbers, so that I can contact them quickly individually if neccessary.

When I receive messages from learners (paper or e-mail) I reply quickly, if only to acknowledge receipt of the messages, and to arrange further communication.

I ensure that course handbooks contain information on how best to communicate with lecturers, and how learners can ensure that messages get back to themselves.

I check that learners know where their 'pigeon holes' are in the department, and follow up instances of mail that has been there unattended for some time.

I encourage learners to use e-mail where they know that the recipient regularly logs-on to the system and replies promptly.

I prepare my own class 'update' sheets, to ensure that my own learners are kept up to date with hand-in dates, assignment briefings, assessment schemes and social events.

I do this often	I do this from time to time	I can do this when needed	I can't yet do this	I'd like to be able to do this	I don't intend to do this	I don't need to do this	Action plans or comments

49 Keeping good records
(this is another checklist for angels and saints!)

I keep my records up to date by attending to them regularly, for example at the end of each week.

I keep all my records in an efficient and easy-to-manage filing system.

I circulate papers quickly to others, and avoid hanging on to them till they're out of date.

I keep copies of important documents in a safe place.

I save on disk rather than keeping photocopies whenever possible, to avoid excessive wastage of paper.

I backup all my disks regularly.

Even if I have not stored things in a tidy way, I know where everything is.

I regularly review the contents of my filing cabinets and remove dross.

I regularly review and make available to students all records about them kept on computer, in compliance with the Data Protection Act.

I inform at least one other person about my system so that things can be located by other people in an emergency.

I do this often	I do this from time to time	I can do this when needed	I can't yet do this	I'd like to be able to do this	I don't intend to do this	I don't need to do this	Action plans or comments

50 Equal opportunities
(this section relates to anti-oppressive practice in all areas, including race, gender, sexuality, age and disability)

I check that I am not treating learners differently in lectures, whatever their background, when I ask questions or let learners give comments.

I regularly interrogate my own practice to avoid oppressive behaviour, and enlist the help of sensitive colleagues to give me feedback on this aspect of my work.

I make efforts to be able to pronounce the names of students with names unfamiliar to me, without any hesitation or insecurity.

In designing case-studies or scenarios, I ensure that I am not typecasting roles according to race, gender, sexuality, age or disability.

I am sensitive to instances where colleagues violate equal-opportunities principles, and bring such occasions to their notice.

I do not use jokes or anecdotes which could be interpreted as oppressive to any group.

I encourage learners to confront issues of inequality objectively, and to work out practical and viable solutions.

I seek feedback from learners to probe any feelings they have regarding being treated unequally in any respect.

I proactively seek to work collaboratively with colleagues of different race, gender, sexuality, age and ability.

I censure any learners who display inappropriate bias in things they say or write.

I do this often	I do this from time to time	I can do this when needed	I can't yet do this	I'd like to be able to do this	I don't intend to do this	I don't need to do this	Action plans or comments

51 Continuing to learn about learning

I keep myself up to date with new developments in teaching and learning.

I regularly read articles, papers and books about the processes and practices of teaching and learning in higher education.

I belong to a professional network for the development of teaching and learning in my subject area.

I belong to a professional association concerned with teaching and learning (such as SEDA (Staff and Educational Development Association), SRHE (Society for Research in Higher Education)).

I attend conferences and staff-development workshops about teaching, learning and assessment.

I contribute actively to conferences and workshops about teaching, learning and assessment.

I write materials for publication on teaching, learning or assessment in my subject area.

I write up and/or discuss with colleagues the successes and problems with innovations I try out in my own teaching and assessment.

I engage in research into the processes of teaching, learning and assessment in my subject area, and monitor the relative effectiveness of different approaches and techniques.

I am continuing my own professional development through an appropriate accreditation scheme, such as Postgraduate Certificate or Diploma, or SEDA accreditation.

I do this often	I do this from time to time	I can do this when needed	I can't yet do this	I'd like to be able to do this	I don't intend to do this	I don't need to do this	Action plans or comments

52 Identifying personal strengths and weaknesses

I identify my strengths, and do not diminish their value by 'shrugging them off'.

For each of my strengths, I collect and/or keep evidence to back up their existence and validity.

I seek out my weaknesses, and try to determine exactly what effects they have on my work.

For each of my weaknesses, I actively explore which strategies I may use to counteract them, or to avoid them affecting my work.

I endeavour to perceive weaknesses as opportunities for future development, rather than as failures.

I regularly appraise and evaluate the opportunities for development available to me.

I prioritize development opportunities, and proactively seek to follow the most relevant ones (for example by making use of training programmes).

I reflect on the threats to my professional performance, and any effects they may have on my work.

I establish the ownership of any threats to my performance, and concentrate on addressing those that lie within my personal reach.

Where I can do something positive about it, I regard a threat as an opportunity for personal development.

I do this often	I do this from time to time	I can do this when needed	I can't yet do this	I'd like to be able to do this	I don't intend to do this	I don't need to do this	Action plans or comments

53 Developing personal scholarship

I actively follow the published research literature in at least one of the disciplines I teach regularly.

I bring to the specialist areas of my teaching the latest ideas from the current research literature on these topics.

I contribute to the design of the curriculum for those subjects where I have a detailed insight, so that the curriculum is as up to date and detailed as is appropriate for learners.

I belong to specialist interest groups or societies in the area of my research, and contribute to them, and exchange ideas and materials with colleagues in other institutions.

I continue to write and publish in my own area of expertise, and use my work in the field to support my teaching in this area.

I develop new specialist interests in further areas which I become involved in through my teaching, and establish contacts specializing in these areas elsewhere.

I share with learners my knowledge of the processes and approaches that are useful in research and scholarship, and encourage them to exploit them in their projects.

I systematically keep references to advances in my specialist field, using a card-index system, or on computer disk.

From time to time, I use library search facilities to check that I have not missed important new contributions to my field in other parts of the world.

I arrange to attend major conferences in my specialist subject area, and aim to contribute actively whenever I can.

I do this often	I do this from time to time	I can do this when needed	I can't yet do this	I'd like to be able to do this	I don't intend to do this	I don't need to do this	Action plans or comments

54 Preparing to be appraised

I am confident in my own mind what I want to get out of the appraisal process.

I identify and make available relevant evidence of my achievement for consideration in my appraisal.

I check that I am familiar with the institutional documentation which indicates the ways in which I need to demonstrate my performance.

For each period of appraisal, I thoroughly review my experiences of my own performance.

I actively consider ways to encourage upward appraisal of my own performance from colleagues working for me or with me.

I am honest with myself about my successes and failures, my strengths and my weaknesses, and about the dimensions of my work that I see as opportunities or threats.

I set out my objectives for the coming year in ways that are achievable, specific and measurable, and am realistic in working out my objectives.

I compare my own objectives and goals with the specified plans of my department and institution.

I work out and specify the evidence I intend to accumulate to demonstrate that I will have both met my objectives, and contributed to the aims of my department.

I decide what staff development programmes I can use to help me achieve my goals and objectives.

I do this often	I do this from time to time	I can do this when needed	I can't yet do this	I'd like to be able to do this	I don't intend to do this	I don't need to do this	Action plans or comments

55 Planning for future development

I consider relevant staff development opportunities, and training options for the coming year.

I take opportunities to gain expertise and experience in chairing and servicing meetings.

I look for publishing opportunities, and/or opportunities to present my work at conferences.

I select and retain evidence to use when seeking promotion or in the context of performance-related pay.

I look for opportunities to work-shadow colleagues in senior posts, or deputize for them when the occasion arises.

I say 'no' firmly and politely to requests to undertake more than a fair share of dull or repetitive duties.

I take time to study new topics which one day I may wish to teach, or which it may be necessary for me to teach at short notice when deputizing for colleagues.

I maintain and build up a list of contacts in my field in other institutions (for example by finding kindred spirits at conferences).

I exchange teaching and learning materials and ideas with contacts in other institutions.

I identify my own personal development targets and goals, and discuss them with colleagues.

I do this often	I do this from time to time	I can do this when needed	I can't yet do this	I'd like to be able to do this	I don't intend to do this	I don't need to do this	Action plans or comments

Taking stock of your teaching and your plans

Finally, we invite you to use the next two pages to summarize your own thinking on issues raised by the contents of this book, and to crystallize your own plans for developing the quality of your teaching.

1 Consolidation

What has using these grids confirmed that I already know about my own teaching quality?

2 Extension

What might I now usefully do more of, or differently, or to a higher level?

3 Enhancement

What do I now need to work on to improve the quality of what I do?

4 Innovation

What might I do instead of things I now do, or how could I make more radical developments to things I already do?

5 Action points

What specific actions or strategies will I undertake to do or try out? (Try to give a commitment to yourself on *what* you will do, *why* you will do it, *how* you will try it, and *by when* you will aim to implement it.)

6 Evaluation

Please cut out or photocopy these two pages and send them directly to either of the authors. How could this book be improved? How could it be used in different and better ways than those we suggested at the beginning? (We thank you in advance for your feedback, and will be pleased to acknowledge your ideas in our next edition.)

Appendix: The SEDA Scheme

Using this book to help you provide evidence for the SEDA 'Accreditation of Teachers in Higher Education' scheme

SEDA, the Staff and Educational Development Association, has set up a scheme by which programmes of training for teachers in higher education can be recognized, with individual teachers who successfully complete such courses being accredited. In order to achieve this, lecturers are required to produce portfolios of evidence to demonstrate their achievement of seven underpinning principles and values, and of eight objectives and outcomes.

For those who are putting together a portfolio, this book can help you to evaluate your effectiveness as a lecturer, and here we indicate where best our checklists may be useful in putting together your evidence.

The SEDA scheme

Underpinning principles and values

Accredited teachers are required to show how these principles and values underpin their work:

1 **How students learn**
   Checklists 3, 4, 10, 11, 13, 15, 16, 18, 20, 25, 26, 27, 31, 38.

2 **Individual difference**
   Checklists 1, 3, 5, 6, 14, 20, 21, 22, 23, 25, 29, 32, 33, 34, 35, 36, 39, 40.

3 **Development**
   Checklists 5, 7, 14, 17, 20, 21, 22, 23, 26, 28, 37, 38.

4 **Scholarship**
   Checklists 14, 15, 16, 17, 18, 42, 45, 51, 53.

5 **Collaborative working**
   Checklists 17, 18, 24, 41, 42, 43, 44, 45, 46, 47, 49.

6 **Equal opportunities**
   Checklists 24, 31, 32, 33, 35, 36, 44, 45, 46, 50.

7 **Reflection**
   The whole book, particularly the final section, but especially Checklists 18, 19, 22, 23, 46, 47, 52, 54, 55.

Objectives and outcomes

Accredited teachers will be required to show how they have:

1   **Designed a teaching programme from a course outline, document or syllabus**
    Checklists 1, 2, 4, 10, 11, 12, 13, 14, 15, 16, 19, 20, 37, 38, 41.

2   **Used a wide and appropriate range of teaching and learning methods, effectively and efficiently, to work with large groups, small groups and one-to-one**
    Checklists 1, 2, 5, 6, 9, 10, 11, 13, 24, 25, 26, 31, 41.

3   **Provided support to students on academic and pastoral matters**
    Checklists 4, 7, 21, 22, 24, 25, 32, 33, 34, 40, 48.

4   **Used a wide range of assessment techniques to assess student work and to enable students to monitor their own progress**
    Checklists 4, 21, 22, 23, 26, 27, 28, 29, 30, 36, 37, 38, 39.

5   **Used a range of self, peer and student monitoring and evaluation techniques**
    Checklists 2, 14, 15, 19, 29, 34, 42, 51, 52, 54, 55.

6   **Performed effectively the teaching and support and academic administration tasks involved in their teaching in their department in the institution**
    Checklists 7, 10, 11, 12, 13, 18, 30, 37, 39, 40, 42, 44, 45, 48, 49, 53.

7   **Developed personal and professional coping strategies within the constraints and opportunities of their institutional setting**
    Checklists 24, 31, 42, 43, 45, 46, 47, 51, 54, 55.

8   **Reflected on their own personal and professional practice and development needs and made a plan for their continuing professional development**
    The whole book, particularly the final section, but especially Checklists 18, 28, 46, 47, 50, 51, 52, 53, 54, 55.

If you wish to know more about the scheme, please contact SEDA at Gala House, 3 Raglan Road, Edgbaston, Birmingham B5 7RA.

Further Reading

There is a vast and varied literature on factors relating to the quality of teaching and learning. The list below comprises only a selection from the available literature, concentrating on books where active learning is a main theme. We think these works will be helpful to those looking for practical ways to improve or enhance their own teaching quality.

Boud, D (ed) (1988) *Developing Student Autonomy in Learning* Kogan Page, London.

Bourner, T and Barlow, J (1991) *The Student Induction Handbook – Practical Activities for Use with New Student Groups* Kogan Page, London.

Bourner, T and Race, P (1991) *How to Win as a Part-Time Student* Kogan Page, London.

Brown, S and Knight, P (1994) *Assessing Learners in Higher Education* Kogan Page, London.

Brown, S, Rust, P and Gibbs, G (1994) *Strategies for Diversifying Assessment in Higher Education* Oxford Centre for Staff Development, Oxford.

Ellington, H I, Percival, F and Race, P (1993) *A Handbook of Educational Technology* (3rd edition) Kogan Page, London.

Ellington, H I and Race, P (1993) *Producing Teaching Materials* (2nd edition) Kogan Page, London.

Gibbs, G, Habeshaw, S and Habeshaw, T (1989) *53 Interesting Ways to Assess Your Students* TES, Bristol.

Gibbs, G and Jenkins, A (eds) (1992) *Teaching Large Classes in Higher Education* Kogan Page, London.

Jaques, D (1991) *Learning in Groups* (2nd edition) Kogan Page, London.

Kemp, R and Race, P (1992) *Promoting the Development of Personal and Professional Skills* CVCP Universities Staff Development Unit, Sheffield.

Lockwood, F (1992) *Activities in Self-Instructional Text* Kogan Page, London.

Morgan, A (1993) *Improving Your Students' Learning: Reflections on the Experience of Study* Kogan Page, London.

Newble, D and Cannon, R (1991) *A Handbook for Teachers in Universities and Colleges* Kogan Page, London.

Race, P (1992) *53 Interesting Ways to Write Open Learning Materials* TES, Bristol.

Race, P (1992) *500 Tips for Students* SCED/Blackwell, Oxford.

Race, P (1994) *Never Mind the Teaching, Feel the Learning* SEDA Paper 80, Birmingham.

Race, P (1994) *The Open Learning Handbook* (2nd edition) Kogan Page, London.

Race, P and Brown, S (1993) *500 Tips for Tutors* Kogan Page, London.

Ramsden, P (1992) *Learning to Teach in Higher Education* Routledge, London.

Rowntree, D (1989) *Assessing Students – How Shall We Know Them?* (revised 2nd edition) Kogan Page, London.

Rowntree, D (1992) *Exploring Open and Distance Learning* Kogan Page, London.

Stephenson, J and Weil, S (eds) (1992) *Quality in Learning* Kogan Page, London.

Webb, G (1994) *Making the Most of Appraisal* Kogan Page, London.

Further details of sources of useful publications

SEDA Publications SEDA produces and distributes a wide range of practical and accessible resource materials for lecturers, in A4 format, on issues around teaching, learning and assessment. For a full list write to SEDA, Gala House, 3 Raglan Road, Edgbaston, Birmingham B5 7RA.

OCSD Publications The Oxford Centre for Staff Development publishes a range of resource materials for lecturers on topics including the teaching and assessment of large groups, resource-based learning, and much more. For details write to Oxford Centre for Staff Development, 75 London Road, Headington, Oxford OX3 9AA.

The '53' series Mostly written by Graham Gibbs, Sue Habeshaw and Trevor Habeshaw, but with several other contributors, these are extremely practical guides to making your teaching more user-friendly and stimulating. Rare is the lecturer who cannot use at least some of the ideas in these books! For the latest list of the books in this series, write to TES, 37 Ravenswood Road, Bristol BS6 6BW.